Annie McGarry

SMITHMARK
PUBLISHERS INC.

4

This edition published in 1993
by SMITHMARK Publishers, Inc.,
16 East 32nd Street,
New York, New York 10016.

SMITHMARK books are available for bulk purchase for sales promotion and premium use. For details write or telephone the Manager of Special Sales, SMITHMARK Publishers Inc., 16 East 32nd Street, New York, NY 10016. (213) 532-6600.

Produced by Brompton Books Corp.,
15 Sherwood Place,
Greenwich, CT 06830.

ISBN 0-8317-5401-X

Printed in Hong Kong

10 9 8 7 6 5 4 3 2 1

Lucy! is dedicated to Donna Marie Armenta, whose only hero in life is Lucille Ball.

Page 1: *Lucy will go to any length—or depth—to break into show business, including going down into the New York City sewer system.*

Page 2: *During a rare break from her busy filming schedule, Lucy peeks out from beneath a sun umbrella.*

CONTENTS

Getting The Ball Rolling

Lucille Ball was born 6 August 1911 in Jamestown, New York. Her father died of typhoid when she was only four, so she moved with her mother, De-De, to Celeron, New York to live with her maternal grandfather, Fred Hunt, and her first cousin, Cleo. Grandpa Hunt introduced his 'Lucyball' (the family nickname) to vaudeville, and remained one of Lucy's biggest supporters, encouraging her to stay in show business even when her acting teacher told her to give up.

Lucy held a number of jobs from the time she was 10 years old, such as selling hot dogs and popcorn at an amusement park, and guiding a blind man while both of them sold soap to passersby on the street. Lucy appeared in all the productions that the Elks put on, and organized the neighborhood children to put on shows on top of the chicken coop in her backyard. At school, her mother De-De produced the plays, and Lucy always found the part that would stand out. Lucy recalled, 'I can't remember not wanting to perform.'

Lucy left quite an impression on the small upstate town. She staged a virtually one-woman production of *Charley's Aunt* at the age of 15. Lucy cast the play, directed it, played the lead, sold the tickets, printed the posters and hauled furniture to the school for props and scenery. Soon after, to the horror of the Celeron gossipmill, she quit high school and left for Manhattan, alone and only 15 years old.

Lucy's cousin Cleo—whom De-De had raised as one of her own and who was like a sister to Lucy—later defended De-De's decision to let Lucy go to New York City. 'De-De was never bound by social conventions of the day. She allowed us to express ourselves. She operated on the theory that none of us would ever do anything to disgrace Grandpa Hunt. It was a relationship based on trust.'

At the age of 16, Lucy enrolled in the Anderson-Milton Dramatics School, where she hung in the back of the room watching the star pupil, Bette Davis. After just six weeks, John Murray Anderson told Lucy's mother and Grandpa Hunt that Lucy should, to paraphrase the expression, get a day job—and forget show business.

The morning after she heard Anderson's critique, determined to prove her teacher wrong, Lucy went out and got a job in the chorus of the third road company of *Rio Rita*, a Ziegfeld production. After five weeks of rehearsal, the director told her, 'It's no use, Montana (Lucy's nickname at the time). You're not meant for show business. Why don't you go home?' Young and alone in a strange city, Lucy somehow maintained her courage and drive.

Lucy was fired from three subsequent chorus parts, and then spent some time on Broadway—as a drugstore soda jerk. She studied modeling during this time, and became a model for Hattie Carnegie, the famous dress designer. Lucy called herself Diane Belmont, after the Belmont Park Race Track on Long Island.

Previous page: In the early 1940s, RKO studios wasted the talents of the young Miss Ball (**here in a studio portrait**) in a series of bit parts and B movies. Her career was given more attention by the people at MGM when she switched studios.

Left: Lucy and Desi feuded and reconciled throughout their marriage, providing a lot of gossip for Hedda Hopper and Walter Winchell. They remained best friends after their divorce, and even continued to work together.

Below, left: Lucy (Lucille Ball) and Ida Lupino are tired of cleaning the catch while Ricky (Desi Arnaz) and Howard Duff go fishing. The two guest stars, a real-life husband and wife team like Lucy and Desi, played themselves on **I Love Lucy** in June 1959.

Opposite page: Gale Gordon began working with Lucy in the early 1940s in **Look Who's Laughing**, an RKO movie version of the Fibber McGee and Molly series. On Lucy's CBS radio show **My Favorite Husband**, Gordon played Rudolph Atterbury, the dignified next-door neighbor, from 1948 until 1951. Lucy badly wanted him to portray Fred Mertz, as well, but he was already under contract to do **Our Miss Brooks** with Eve Arden. Gordon did appear on **I Love Lucy** as Ricky's boss at the Tropicana, Alvin Littlefield, in two episodes aired in 1952. Eleven years later, they began an eleven-year association on **The Lucy Show** (1963-1968) and **Here's Lucy** (1968-1974.)

Then, at age 17, Lucy was felled by a case of rheumatoid arthritis. She spent eight months in the hospital with heavy weights on her ankles to straighten her contorted legs, and three years learning to walk again, after which she resumed her modeling career. As the Chesterfield cigarette girl, Lucy's picture was plastered on billboards all over New York for awhile. Later, the same company sponsored *I Love Lucy*.

At 22, Lucy had spent one third of her life trying to break into show business, and yet she seemed no closer to an acting career. That is, until one afternoon when she was walking up Broadway, an agent grabbed her and asked, 'How would you like to go to California?' It seemed that one of the showgirls

chosen for an Eddie Cantor film couldn't go—her mother wouldn't let her. Busby Berkeley picked Lucy out of the line and recommended her to Sam Goldwyn, who balked at first, thinking she had no talent. However, he conceded to Berkeley, who forever after prided himself upon discovering Lucy.

However, Lucy was dissatisfied with her treatment at MGM, insulted by her tiny roles and sick of being 'background.' She wanted desperately to move to Columbia Pictures which specialized in the knockabout sort of comedy in which Lucy excelled.

In 1934, when Lucy was 23 years old, Columbia Pictures signed her to a contract as a stock player at $50 a week. Lucy wired her family and excitedly told them to move out to California and live with her. By the time Lucy's mother, brother Fred, cousin Cleo and Grandpa Hunt had arrived from New York, Columbia had dissolved their stock company, firing everyone, and Lucy was working as an extra for Paramount.

During a three-month stint with the Three Stooges, Lucy did bit parts in movies such as *Moulin Rouge* and *Roberta*. Her appearance in the latter so impressed RKO executives that they signed her to a contract. She did some B movies, and then began working with Jack Oakie, Joe Penner and the Marx Brothers (*Room Service*). With her salary at $1500 a week—and her hair dyed that unforgettable shade of 'strawberry orange'—Lucy landed a part in RKO's *Dance, Girl, Dance*. It was then, in 1939, that she met Desi Arnaz.

Opposite page, above and be-low: *In 1973, Lucy plunged into working on the musical,* **Mame***, based on Patrick Dennis' book,* **Auntie Mame***, and on the Broadway play. Lucy made her role in* **Mame** *look glamorous, while she was working harder than ever before on her dancing and singing.*

At right: *In Tijuana in June 1958, while making the first* **Desilu Playhouse***, Lucy had to fight a real bull. The bull had foot-long horns, but was guaranteed to be docile. Lucy was to wave a perfume-soaked handkerchief at the bull to stop him in his tracks. When a stage hand asked Miss Ball what kind of perfume was on the hanky, she wisecracked, 'Eau de hamburger. That oughta keep him in line.' This ad-lib was then written into the script. While the real bull gave Lucy no trouble, a bull's head that was mounted on wheels and rolled at Lucy at high speeds jumped its tracks and actually gored her, sending a bruised and bat-tered Lucy to the hospital for stitches.*

Below, right: *Lucy with a younger gen-eration of comediennes: Bette Midler (**left**) and Lily Tomlin (**right**).*

Above: By 1951, the happy couple at last had their own television show, complete with this sentimental theme song:

'There's a certain couple that I know.
They're strictly love birds.
A pair of turtle dove birds.
He's a guy who wants the world to know,
So ev'ry day you'll hear him say:
I love Lucy and she loves me.
We're as happy as two can be.
Sometimes we quarrel but then
How we love making up again.
Lucy kisses like no one can.
She's my missus and I'm her man.
And life is heaven, you see,
Cause I love Lucy,
Yes, I love Lucy
And Lucy loves me.'

Composed by Harold Adamson for the occasion of Lucy Ricardo's birthday (telecast 11 May 1953), Ricky sang the words to the **I Love Lucy** theme song only once.

Opposite page: The effervescent Miss Ball, beautiful as well as talented.

He Loves Lucy

Desiderio Alberto Arnaz y de Acha III was the only child of a Cuban senator and mayor of Santiago, Cuba. Desi had at his disposal all that his family owned: 100,000 acres, many homes, boats, cars, an island retreat and a stable of racehorses. The family's plan had been for Desi to go to the University of Notre Dame in South Bend, Indiana, to get a law degree and return home to the practice awaiting him.

By his own admission, Desi was spoiled; in his words, he was a 'fathead'. Fate stepped in to strengthen Desi's character, however, in the form of the Batista revolution on 12 August 1933, when Desi was only 16 years old. Desi's father was jailed and their property confiscated. Desi and his mother fled to Miami, where Desi worked at odd jobs, including bird cage-cleaning. He eventually won a place with the Siboney Septet as a singer. Desi said, 'I don't know why it was called a septet since there were only five of us. I guess septet sounded better.'

After a series of gigs with different bands, he landed in New York, where he was spotted by George Abbott and given a leading role in the new stage musical, *Too Many Girls*. RKO bought the movie rights and cast Desi in the film version.

In the studio commissary, director George Abbott introduced 23-year-old Desi to a young woman who looked, according to Desi, 'awful—very tough. I didn't like her at first.' Lucy was made up to look like a burlesque queen for a role in *Dance, Girl, Dance*. She had a black eye from filming a rough scene with Maureen O'Hara.

Desi could hardly believe it when he was told that this was the actress who would play the guileless young Consuelo Casey in the movie *Too Many Girls*. Desi told the director, 'What kind of girl is this? She's no sweet, ingenue type.'

Desi's opinion changed drastically later that same day when he saw Lucille at a cast briefing. She was wearing a cashmere sweater and a yellow skirt. 'I asked her if she knew how to rumba, and when she said no, I offered to teach her.'

'Some line he had!' Lucy returned. 'We went out all right, but all we did was sit and yak all night. Never got to dance once.'

It was love at second sight, but the studio didn't want them to marry. 'We spent the better part of our courtship telling each other it would hurt our careers,' Desi recalled.

On 29 November 1940, Lucy flew to New York, where Desi was playing with his band at the Roxy Theatre. At the airport, she gave an interview to a reporter whose story's main focus was that Lucy and Desi would never marry. At the end of the interview, Desi shocked both the reporter and Lucy by proposing.

At five o'clock the next morning, the couple drove to Greenwich, Connecticut, and were married five hours later by a justice of the peace at the Byram River Beagle Club.

As they drove back to New York City, news of their wedding was on the car radio. At the Roxy, Desi led Lucy out on stage to explain his absence from the first show. The stage manager had

Lucy could play ingenues (**opposite page**) or cool, tough, bawdy women (**previous page**).

At right: Lucy always enjoyed her forays into radio, and had no intention of leaving her movie career for television until CBS suggested it.

Below: On 30 November 1940, after a five-hour drive to a Connecticut justice of the peace, Lucy and Desi realized that they had forgotten to get blood tests and a wedding ring. While Lucy and Desi rushed to get the tests done, Desi's agent and manager were sent out to find a ring. All the Greenwich jewelers were closed for the weekend, so in desperation, the two men made their way to a five-and-dime store, where they purchased the silliest-looking 10-cent copper wedding ring they could find. Later, Lucy and Desi had the ring coated in platinum.

a surprise for them: he had supplied the elated crowd with rice.

Lucy described the whirlwind romance and wedding as the most impulsive thing she'd ever done. Said Lucy, 'Hollywood gave our marriage six months; I gave it six weeks!'

Their marriage was indeed troubled, primarily by the jealousy and suspicion that came from the fact that they were separated much of the time by their work. Lucy's movie career was taking off. Her role as a paraplegic showgirl in Damon Runyon's *The Big Street* was so convincing that every studio was bidding for her services. On her 31st birthday in 1942, she signed with MGM and won the leading role in *DuBarry Was a Lady* with Gene Kelly.

Meanwhile, Desi's movie career had stalled. He had been in a few movies, but with the exception of *Bataan*, all of them were forgettable. He began to tour with a band again, and the enforced separation from Lucy proved to be an anathema to their marriage.

The marriage received a stay of execution through World War II when Desi was drafted into the infantry. However, a

*At left: **Du Barry Was a Lady** co-starred Red Skelton (**far left**) and Gene Kelly (**far right**), while Zero Mostel appeared as a fortune teller. One film highlight was the Tommy Dorsey Orchestra — including Buddy Rich, Dick Haymes and Jo Stafford — in Louis XV period costumes and wigs.*

*Below: Lucy on the set. In 1943, MGM gave Lucy the opportunity to appear in the film version of Cole Porter's successful stage show, **Du Barry Was a Lady**. Lucy was hesitant, knowing her own limitations where singing and dancing were concerned, and wondering how she could possibly follow in Ethel Merman's footsteps. MGM assigned Lucy a great dance coach, Charles Walters, and Robert Alton, the musical director, to prepare her for the part. She did so well that Louis B Mayer congratulated her personally on her performance.*

*Opposite page: In **Du Barry Was a Lady**, Red Skelton has a dream in which he is King Louis XV, lecherously pursuing Lucy. Dressed in powdered wigs and hoopskirts, Lucy lip-synched to a score of Cole Porter songs such as 'Do I Love You?' and 'Friendship.'*

broken kneecap landed him in Army Special Services, where he guided USO troops from base to base in California.

Soon after his return home, though, Lucy filed for divorce. They fought so often that they had a guest house built out in the backyard for Desi, referred to as 'the doghouse.' The couple were not able to keep apart, however, and eventually reconciled. In order to keep Desi at home for a couple of years, Lucy convinced Bob Hope to sign Desi as the band leader on his NBC radio show. Meanwhile, she was busy on her own radio show, *My Favorite Husband*, co-starring Richard Denning. When CBS approached Lucy with the idea of taking the show to television, with the cast intact, Lucy decided that the best way to keep her marriage together was for her and Desi to work together. She handed the CBS executives her ultimatum: without Desi, there'd be no Lucy.

The producer of *My Favorite Husband*, Jess Oppenheimer, who would also be producing the television show, was in favor of Lucy's real husband playing her husband on the show, but he couldn't convince the advertising people and the sponsors, who felt that viewers wouldn't believe an All-American redhead married to a Cuban bandleader. These obstacles only served to strengthen Lucy's resolve.

In early summer of 1950, Lucy and Desi went on the road to perform live stage shows and prove to CBS that people would love their act. They opened at the Paramount Theatre in Chicago with Desi's band, fantastic costumes and wacky props. Their slapstick routines were built around a famous movie star who tries to join her bandleader husband's act. For their finale, Lucy sang 'Cuban Pete/Sally Sweet' with Desi's band's accompaniment. The reviews were excellent.

The next stop was the Roxy Theatre in New York, where the

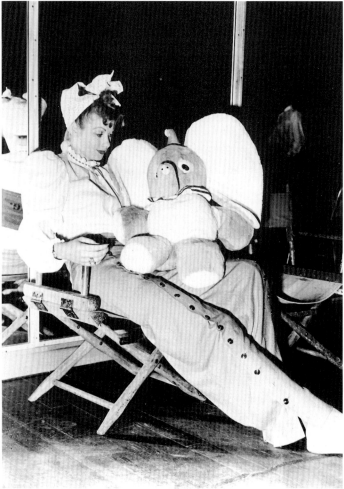

During the early years of Lucy's career, her talents were often wasted in forgettable films. **Opposite page:** *Lucy appeared in* **Two Smart People** *in 1946, one of the five films she made in that year alone. Her co-star was John Hodiak, a serious-looking leading man of the 1940s.*

At right: *Lucy skeptically regards Franchot Tone, who played her husband in* **Her Husband's Affairs**.

Below, right: *Heads roll on the set as Lucy sends Gene Kelly to the guillotine. Karl Freund did the photography on this film, and Lucy looked so gorgeous throughout the production that she hired the Oscar-winning cinematographer to direct the photography on* **I Love Lucy**.

reviews echoed those they had received in Chicago. They celebrated their tenth wedding anniversary several months prematurely on 13 June 1950, in the same dressing room suite over whose threshold Desi had carried Lucy after their Greenwich, Connecticut ceremony.

As the tour went on, Lucy complained of chronic tiredness, but both she and Desi put it down to their heavy performance schedule. When she began to feel ill, she went to a doctor, who asked her, 'Do you think you might be pregnant?' Lucy hadn't even considered this possibility. She had suffered a miscar-

riage in the first year of their marriage, and she and Desi believed that they were unable to have children.

They heard the results of her rabbit test when they turned on the television. A laboratory clerk had leaked the news to Walter Winchell, who then relayed the information to the couple and the rest of the viewing nation.

The expectant parents immediately cancelled the second half of their tour, including the London Palladium, and altered the act to make allowances for Lucy's impending motherhood.
continued on page 24

Above: Lucy cracks the whip over eight chorus girls dressed as panthers in Vincente Minnelli's 1946 musical, **Ziegfeld's Follies.** Lucy, who had actually been a Ziegfeld girl herself, was in good company in a film which featured Judy Garland, Fred Astaire, Fanny Brice, Cyd Charisse, Red Skelton, Lena Horne, Gene Kelly, Hume Cronyn and Esther Williams. Hume Cronyn and Lucy shared the limelight again in 1987, when they were both honored by President Ronald Reagan with lifetime achievement awards (see page 77).

One highlight of this all-star production was a dance number between Fred Astaire and Gene Kelly. It was on this set that Lucy met the future Fred Mertz, William Frawley.

Right: Lucille Ball moved with ease from glamourous star to star-struck housewife.

Bob Hope was a great help to Lucy's career in the early days, convincing Paramount to take a chance on the almost unknown actress for the leading role opposite him in **Sorrowful Jones** (1949). The chemistry between the two comedians was exciting to watch, and the film was a hit, earning twice as much as any other Bob Hope film of the time.

Fancy Pants (1950) (**left**) was a reworking of **Ruggles of Red Gap**, with Bob Hope as a struggling comic actor who poses as an English butler. Through a series of mishaps and misunderstandings, a crude nouveau-riche family hires him and takes him to New Mexico. Lucy played the young heiress who falls in love with the klutzy butler.

On the set, Lucy was teaching Bob Hope how to ride a mechanical horse when suddenly the horse went out of control—'galloping like a two year old in heat,' as Hope put it—throwing Bob flat onto a cement floor. Miraculously, Hope was unhurt, aside from the $4500 doctor bill for therapy, but he never rode a mechanical horse again.

Below, left: Lucy and Franchot Tone appeared in the 1947 film **Her Husband's Affairs**, which foreshadowed **I Love Lucy** in plot: Lucy plays a wife whose husband tries to teach her not to meddle in his business concerns.

Opposite page: Lucy and Richard Denning (**at right**) played Liz and George Cooper on CBS radio's **My Favorite Husband**, a popular series which ran from 1948 to 1951. Lucy played Liz Cooper, a somewhat crazed, klutzy housewife, who was the basis for the character of Lucy Ricardo. Network officials insisted that the team remain together for the television version, but Lucy demanded that she co-star with her own husband, Desi Arnaz.

continued from page 21
Official announcements were made, and the stage was set for Lucy and Desi to have their first child.

On 20 July 1950, Lucy was rushed to Cedars of Lebanon Hospital in Los Angeles, where a team of doctors struggled for a week to save Lucy's baby, and failed. Lucy received almost 3000 letters of condolence from fans.

Three months later, in October 1950, Lucy discovered that she was pregnant again. This time, all her acting engagements were cancelled, except the radio show, which wasn't strenuous. Meanwhile, Lucy and Desi made the announcement that unless they appeared together, Lucy would never act again.

In late December 1950, William S Paley, the president of CBS, refused to underwrite the show, but reluctantly agreed to sell Lucy and Desi airtime if they could finance their show. It would be a huge risk for them monetarily and professionally. Desi was a highly-paid bandleader, and Lucy had a lucrative career in films. All of their friends and colleagues kept reminding them of how much they had to lose.

Finally Lucy had a dream in which her dead friend Carole Lombard appeared to her, urging her, 'Honey, go ahead. Take a chance. Give it a whirl!'

She and Desi borrowed $8000 and became television producers. They called their company Desilu.

At left: In their 1954 movie, **The Long, Long Trailer**, their second full-length movie together, Lucy and Desi exchanged vows for the third time. Of their real life marriage, Lucy said, 'Hollywood gave our marriage six months; I gave it six weeks!'

Below: The Long, Long Trailer was the 'vehicle' to bring Desi's and Lucy's considerable comic talents back to the silver screen. Director Vincente Minnelli brought a charm, ease and grace to this sometimes manic 1954 comedy about a couple who take their honeymoon in an increasingly cumbersome trailer.

At right: An MGM portrait for **The Long, Long Trailer**. Lucy and Desi continued to work together even during their break from **I Love Lucy**.

Break A Leg

The original premise for Desi and Lucy's television show was that Lucy would be a movie star, and Desi a successful band-leader—true to their real, glamorous lives. This idea was rejected as being too far removed from middle America, so they faced the task of developing two characters with whom the average person could identify. Therefore, Lucy became a housewife with show-biz aspirations and Desi a small-time nightclub bandleader at the Tropicana Nightclub in New York City. They lived in a modest brownstone at 623 Sixty-eighth Street, number 4-A. On a map of Manhattan, one discovers that Lucy and Ricky lived in the middle of the East River.

Naming the show proved to be quite a problem. Most sit-coms at the time were named for the star, such as *The George Burns and Gracie Allen Show*. The network wanted to call the show *The Lucille Ball Show—costarring Desi Arnaz*. Lucy became irate at the perceived slight to Desi, and threatened again to quit. They tried *The Lucille Ball and Desi Arnaz Show*. Again Lucy rejected their suggestion, because her name came before her husband's. When someone suggested *I Love Lucy*, Lucy approved because the 'I' referred to Desi.

As the show began to take form, Lucy and Desi were informed by the network that they had to move to New York. Philip Morris, their sponsor, had more smokers east of the Mississippi than west, and so wanted the live transmission to emanate out of New York. Low quality kinescopes, films made of the live airing from a television screen, could then be shown on the western side of the United States.

Lucy and Desi scrambled to come up with a strategy that would allow them to stay in their adopted home state. Their baby was due any day, and Desi had just finished building the baby's room onto the house on the Desilu Ranch in Chatsworth, California. Working with cinematographer Karl Freund, Desi came up with an idea.

Desi proposed that the show be performed like a stage play, in chronological sequence with a live audience watching, and filmed like a motion picture, with four cameras picking up different angles. That way Desi and Lucy could stay in California and send a high quality film to the East Coast. No one had ever filmed a television show before.

Everyone told them that executing the idea would be problematical, if not impossible. The lighting, the presence of an audience on a sound stage—or finding a theatre with a stage wide enough to accomodate three or four sets—were only some of the problems facing Desilu.

Desi asked Karl 'Papa' Freund to be the cinematographer for the show. Desi and Lucy had met Papa in 1943 on the set of *DuBarry Was a Lady*, Lucy's first movie for MGM. Papa had an Oscar to his credit for *The Good Earth* in 1937, had directed three Garbo movies, and was generally known as a genius among those in the industry. Freund had been used to making $75,000 a year in the 1940s at MGM, and Desi would only offer him union scale. Freund was already retired, but when Desi challenged him to develop Desi's brainchild, Papa couldn't refuse.

Previous page: Ricky and Lucy Ricardo and their neighbors, Ethel and Fred Mertz (Vivian Vance and William Frawley).

At left: Lucy and Desi were so determined to work together that they bank-rolled their own show, risking their life savings and their careers in the process. They formed Desilu Productions in 1951 with a $8000 loan, matching the funds with their own money, and set about creating **I Love Lucy**. By 1954, Desilu controlled 229 half-hour shows, and eventually was estimated to be worth $100 million.

Opposite page: Lucy and the neighbors, Ethel and Fred Mertz. Fred's cutting remarks to Ethel, his wife on the show, were not far from Frawley's actual off-camera demeanor toward his co-star, Vivian Vance. He once said of her, 'She's one of the finest gals to come out of Kansas, but I often wish she'd go back there. I don't know where she is now and she doesn't know where I am and that's exactly the way I like it.'

Frawley, a great baseball fan, had a clause written into his contract that if the New York Yankees won the American League pennant, he would be free to go to the World Series. That seemingly insignificant stipulation caused Desilu Productions a lot of grief during the run of **I Love Lucy**. The Yankees took Bill Frawley away from the set seven out of nine seasons.

On 17 July 1951, Desi and Lucy's child was born Lucie Desiree Arnaz. Desi wrote a song, 'There's a Brand New Baby at Our House,' which he sang two years later on I Love Lucy upon the arrival of Little Ricky.

The Couple Next Door

William Frawley, a film actor since 1931, heard about the role of Fred Mertz from his agent. He called Lucille Ball and asked her point-blank if she needed a good actor to play the part of Fred. Lucy consulted with Desi, and they agreed that Frawley had been wonderful in the films Mother Wore Tights, Miracle on 34th Street and others. Born in 1887, Frawley started in vaudeville at the age of 21 against the wishes of his worried mother. He traveled the vaudeville circuit until 1927, when he began appearing in hundreds of movies. Frawley had a good résumé, but the CBS officials were not optimistic. They warned the new producers that the 64-year-old Frawley was known for his dour temperament and his drinking.

Desi met with Frawley and hired him with one stipulation: one absence without a legitimate medical excuse and Frawley was off the show. Frawley, railing about the CBS officials and downing scotches, insisted that he had no drinking problem.

The part of Ethel was a difficult one to cast, because she had to be someone who audiences would believe was married to an old coot like Fred Mertz. Up for a film at Universal Studios at the time, Vivian Vance was not interested in doing television, but her old friend, Marc Daniels, the director, finally convinced her to join the cast.

Vance was born in Cherryvale, Kansas on 26 July 1912. Like Lucy, people tried to discourage her from show business. A casting agent once told Vance to go home because her eyes were set too close together. She didn't take his advice, however, and went on to great success in theatre. She spent her spare hours singing in nightclubs. She went on to do several films, but in 1945, Vance suffered a nervous breakdown, from which it took her years to recover. When given the chance to be in I Love Lucy, she was appearing — at the insistence of her concerned husband — in her first play since her breakdown.

It's Showtime

A quarter of a million dollars had been spent on the first episode of I Love Lucy. The careers of the two principal actors — as well as their marriage — were at stake, as was the position of their champion at CBS, Harry Ackerman.

Above: In an episode entitled 'Lucy Tells the Truth,' (originally aired 9 November 1953) Lucy bets Ricky and the Mertzes that she can go 24 hours without telling even a white lie. At Caroline Appleby's bridge game, however, Lucy says what she **really** thinks of the Appleby's new Chinese modern furniture and of Marion's new hat and loud laugh (Lucy: 'Marion, stop cackling. I've been waiting 10 years for you to lay that egg!'). Then Lucy must truthfully answer their questions about her age (Lucy Ricardo is 33 yearsold; at the time, Lucille Ball was 42,) weight (129 pounds) and original hair color (mousy brown).

Later, Ricky takes her to a television show audition, where Lucy must answer the casting director's questions about previous experience. Lucy replies that she has just finished an 11-year run at Ricardo's, 'a three-ring circus,' and has appeared in 3-D (the Ricardos' apartment number). Lucy wins the audition, and becomes the lovely assistant to Professor Falconi, the knife-thrower, thereby winning $100 from Ricky and the Mertzes.

At right: *While Ricky Ricardo refused to let his wife have a career, Desi Arnaz and his wife became partners, and together they created a multi-million dollar production company. Lucy's previously untapped potential as a businesswoman was put to excellent use in the running of Desilu. Years later, after buying out Desi's half of the corporation, Lucille Ball proved a formidable CEO.*

Below, right: *The 'Vitameatavegamin' episode, in which Lucy accidentally becomes drunk while making a commercial, is considered a classic. Character actor Ross Elliott played the television director. Elliott said, 'I chewed the inside of my mouth to keep from laughing out loud. Lucy would do new stuff that wasn't rehearsed, like an extra funny face. Then, at one point, she became 'drunk' and started making eyes at me, flirting, and I almost broke up again.'*

A laser disk released in 1991 featured two half-hour shows: this and the show in which Lucy gets a job in a candy factory, which has become virtually the signature episode of the series.

They should not have worried. The studio audience convulsed with laughter for the duration of the 30-minute first episode. Called 'The Diet,' the première found poor Lucy faced with losing 12 pounds in four days in order to fit into a tiny costume for a routine at the Tropicana. The audience roared as Lucy rolled on the floor with a dog for a scrap of meat, and went wild when Lucy and Desi reprised some of the songs from their vaudeville tour from 14 months earlier.

Desi and Lucy still had their doubts, however. Not convinced by the audience's laughter, they continued to preview the film of 'The Diet' at theatres and with makeshift audiences on the sound stage. They felt that the reaction wasn't judgmental enough. Ten days later, on Monday, 15 October 1951, *I Love Lucy* made its debut. Despite some popular shows scheduled against them in the nine o'clock time slot, the show seemed destined to be a hit.

'The Diet' was not the first show aired. Because of its technical difficulties, Jess Oppenheimer, the head writer and one of the show's three creators, chose for the première the episode filmed third. Entitled 'The Girls Want to Go to a Nightclub,' the show's CBS press release went as follows:

'When the curtain rises, Ricky and Fred are plotting to attend the boxing matches despite the announced plans of the wives to go nightclubbing in celebration of Fred and Ethel's wedding anniversary.

'When the girls refuse to go to the fights, the boys arrange for a pair of blind dates. Later Lucy and Ethel deck themselves out as a couple of hillbillies to substitute for the blind dates.'

Time magazine wrote, '... [W]hat televiewers see on screen is the sort of cheerful rowdiness that has been rare in the US since the days of the silent movies' Keystone Comedies. Lucille submits enthusiastically to being hit with pies; she falls over furniture, gets locked in home freezers, is chased by knife-wielding fanatics. Tricked out as a ballerina or a Hindu maharanee or a

At left: *Ball keeps her eye on the boys. As time went by, the budget increased, and more elaborate costumes were used.*

Below, left: *Vivian Vance harbored some resentment for Lucille, because—though she was actually a year younger than Lucille Ball—her contract mandated that she appear frumpier than the star. She was contractually committed to remaining 20 pounds overweight, and her wardrobe—until she demanded control of it—consisted of frowsy housedresses.*

Vance, tired of disguising her own natural attractiveness, was reluctant to stay with the show when it switched to the hour-long format, but she was given liberties with the increased budget to buy herself a new wardrobe.

Opposite page: *Writers Madelyn Pugh and Bob Carroll, Jr, inspired by Lucille Ball's love of bop music, wrote an episode in which Lucy plays 'Glow Worm' on the saxophone.*

toothless hillbilly, she takes her assorted lumps and pratfalls with unflagging zest and good humor. Her mobile, rubbery face reflects a limitless variety of emotions, from maniacal pleasure to sepulchral gloom. Even on a flickering, pallid TV screen, her wide-set, saucer eyes beam with the massed candlepower of a lighthouse on a dark night.'

Desilu Productions was off and gunning for the number one show in television.

Little Ricky and Desi, Jr

In the show's second season, Lucy and Desi discovered that they were expecting another baby. At first they panicked, thinking that the show would have to be cancelled. Pregnancy was not regarded as a fit subject for a situation comedy at the time. Then they reconsidered, deciding that Lucy and Ricky Ricardo

would have a baby as well. Three religious leaders were given advance scripts and special sneak previews to make sure that the shows would not offend anyone. The monsignor, the rabbi and the Presbyterian reverend all agreed: What is objectionable about having a baby?

The news was announced in an episode entitled, 'Lucy is Enceinte'—Spanish for pregnant. While 207 letters were received protesting the use of pregnancy as a subject for a comedy show, almost 30,000 arrived to congratulate Lucy and Desi. The couple eventually received over a million indications of public support, including phone calls, telegrams and gifts. The booties, blankets and bonnets had to be hauled away by the truckload, donated by the Arnazes to state instituions.

Desi, Lucy, Jess Oppenheimer and the other writers had decided that the Ricardo baby would be a boy, regardless of the Arnaz baby's sex. The reason given for this was a muddled

continued on page 38

At left: In the scene in which Lucy tells Ricky of her pregnancy, the script read that Desi was supposed to shout with joy. Instead, as the three cameras rolled, he broke down and cried.

Below: Vivian and Lucy liked one another immediately, and despite frequent arguments on the set, had great affection for each other. Years after Vivian's death in 1979, the mention of her name could still bring tears to Lucy's eyes.

Opposite page: The writers incorporated a lot of the couple's own history into the Ricardo chronicles. Both the Ricardos and the Arnazes were married in 1940 at the Byram River Beagle Club in Greenwich, Connecticut. Both couples renewed their vows after nine years.

The ultimate imitation of real life, however, came when Lucille Ball and Lucy Ricardo delivered babies on the same day.

continued from page 34

At left: A jealous Lucy dreams one night that she and Little Ricky are left in the lurch by Ricky because of a new singer. In the dream, she and Little Ricky wait for years outside the Tropicana for Ricky to come out.

Below, left: Keith Thibodeaux, 'The World's Tiniest Professional Drummer,' **far left**, played Little Ricky for the 1956 to 1957 season. The moment Desi saw five-year-old Keith (born 1 December 1950), he signed him to a seven year contract at $300 a week. Keith was given Spanish lessons, and he was raised alongside Desi, Jr. His name was changed to Richard (Ricky) Keith. Keith's drumming and acting talent was shown to its best advantage in these episodes: 'Little Ricky Learns to Play the Drums' and 'Little Ricky Gets Stage Fright.'

In 'The Ricardos Visit Cuba,' Keith and Desi, Sr do a conga drum duet. Young Keith complained because everyone called him Desi; Desi, Jr was confused because people called him Little Ricky. Though Keith was two years older than Desi, and despite a strange 'sibling' rivalry, the two became best friends.

Opposite page: When the Ricardos moved to Hollywood, it gave the writers the perfect opportunity to write some of Lucy's and Desi's famous friends into the script. During the years 1955 to 1958, Betty Grable, Harry James, William Holden, Eve Arden, Hedda Hopper, Rock Hudson, Van Johnson, Fred MacMurray, Tallulah Bankhead, Ann Sothern, Cesar Romero, Rudy Vallee, Maurice Chevalier, Harpo Marx (**pictured**), Cornel Wilde, Richard Widmark, Danny Thomas and John Wayne all appeared on the show.

explanation concerning little Lucie. Supposedly, the 18-month-old would be confused by another little girl on the screen with her mommy and daddy. The truth was that Desi so desperately wanted a boy in real life that he was determined to have a son on television, at least.

The morning of Monday, 19 January 1953, Lucy went into Cedars-Lebanon Hospital in Los Angeles and delivered Desiderio Alberto Arnaz y de Acha IV by cesarean section. Throughout the operation, she kept demanding that the doctor tell her the sex of the baby. When at last she heard that her baby was a boy, she said, 'Desi will be so happy,' and promptly fell asleep. Desi was indeed happy. He immediately got on the phone to Jess Oppenheimer, yelling, 'Lucy followed your script! Ain't she something?'

'Terrific!' replied Oppenheimer. 'That makes me the greatest writer in the world. Tell Lucy she can take the rest of the day off.'

That night, 44 million viewers watched the episode entitled, 'Lucy Goes to the Hospital,' with an incredible 71.7 percent

At left: When the Mertzes and the Ricardos travel through Europe together, Lucy and Ethel spy handsome Charles Boyer at an outdoor café in Paris. While they run off to powder their noses, Ricky and Fred warn Boyer about their wives. When Lucy returns, Boyer tells her that he is a struggling actor, Maurice DuBois, who is frustrated because he is always getting mistaken for the famous actor. Later that day, Lucy reads in the paper that Ricky has a meeting with Boyer. When she begs Ricky to take her along, Ricky feigns jealousy.

To prove her loyalty to Ricky, Lucy finds 'Maurice DuBois' and hires him to portray Charles Boyer—of whom he can, of course, do a convincing impersonation—and to flirt with her in Ricky's presence while she ignores him. Ethel tips Lucy off that DuBois **is** Boyer and Lucy becomes completely unglued. The original airing of this episode was 5 March 1956.

Below, left and opposite: The Mertzes and the Ricardos go to Sun Valley, Idaho in an episode originally aired 14 April 1958. Fernando Lamas (**standing**) played the flirtatious ski instructor. Fortunately, a double was used for Lucille Ball in the skiing scene—the double broke her leg.

share of the audience, while only 29 million watched the presidential inauguration of Dwight David Eisenhower the following night. Desi commented that he wanted to run Lucy for president in 1956.

After Little Ricky's birth, CBS and the Arnazes renegotiated their deal, and the series was guaranteed life through the next two-and-a-half years. The weekly budget for the program was upped from $19,500 to between $40,000 and $50,000. The merchandising tie-ins alone were estimated to be worth $50 million: a 'Ricky, Jr' doll, clothes such as 'Desi Denims' and 'Lucy Lingerie,' linens, and even a coffee table 'just like the one in the Ricardos' living room.'

Opposite page: *A Buckingham Palace guard tries to keep from smiling in the face of Lucy's antics.*

At right: *Vivian Vance, her husband Phil Ober, Lucy and Fernando Lamas take a break during the filming of the European shows.*

The show had already been through several different story lines: Lucy trying to break into show business; Lucy and Desi having husband-and-wife squabbles; and then along came Little Ricky, providing a fresh source for material. In their third season, however, the writing staff felt that they had already exhausted these story lines and didn't know quite where to turn for new ideas. They decided to move the Ricardos from New York City to Hollywood for the fourth season, where Ricky wins a screen test and a studio offer. This plot twist would give plenty of opportunity for real stars to come on the show and play themselves. In all, 27 episodes, filmed between 1955 and 1957, featured the Ricardos in Hollywood.

Lucy and Desi had great appreciation for their writers — Jess Oppenheimer, Madelyn Pugh and Bob Carroll, Jr — who often worked more than 70 hours a week. At the party celebrating the 100th episode of *I Love Lucy*, Lucille Ball gave tribute to the three people who had helped make the show number one. 'I love them dearly,' she said. 'I appreciate them daily, I praise them hourly, and I thank God for them every night.' Desi gave Jess Oppenheimer a baseball statuette, with a punning tribute, 'To the man behind the ball.'

Writer Madelyn Pugh not only wrote the skits along with partner Bob Carroll, Jr, she would also attempt them herself, to be sure that Lucy could do them. In the line of duty, Madelyn was rolled up in a rug, carted off in a garbage can, and had her head stuck in a loving cup. She filled her blouse with eggs, glued icicles to her face, and tried wrapping chocolate bonbons at breakneck speed.

In 1957, Desi negotiated with CBS chief William S Paley to end the half-hour *I Love Lucy* shows, and create a new hour-long format which would be shown every other week. Paley even offered him $80,000 a week to stick with the half-hour format, and $30,000 for each rerun. At the time, the going price for a sitcom was only $48,000, but Desi turned Paley down.

In the spring of 1957, the Ford Motor Company sponsored *The Lucille Ball-Desi Arnaz Show*, five, one-hour color specials, each with a budget of $350,000 — quite a figure compared to the $19,500 for the original half-hour shows. The budget would go to lavish sets, celebrity guest stars and shootings at exotic locations.

In the opening scene of *The Lucille Ball-Desi Arnaz Show*, set in the Ricardo's Westport, Connecticut home, Hedda Hopper questions the couple about how they met. A flashback takes the viewers back 16 years to a cruise ship bound for Cuba. Lucy MacGillicudy and Susie McNamara — Ann Sothern playing her character from *Private Secretary* — are two stenographers on vacation. They meet newlyweds Fred — with hair — and Ethel Mertz, and singer Rudy Vallee. Once in Havana, the girls meet two local taxi drivers — Ricky Ricardo and his buddy Carlos (Cesar Romero), who conduct sight-seeing tours. Ricky's dream, however, is to come to America and be a musician. Lucy and Ricky have a whirlwind romance, and the rest is sitcom history.

An episode entitled 'Lucy Hunts Uranium,' starring Fred MacMurray, called for a car to drive at high speeds and come to a stop right before the cameras. Desi's frustration mounted as the stunt man drove the car out of camera range, take after take. Finally, Desi jumped into driver's seat and performed the stunt perfectly on the first try. The car stopped right in front of the cameras, and Desi triumphantly leaped out, only to be told by *continued on page 46*

Opposite page: Lucy is in trouble with Ricky again, with Danny Thomas in the middle. Danny appeared on **I Love Lucy** in December 1958 as Danny Williams, his character from his own television series, **Make Room For Daddy**.

Above: In 'Lucy's Summer Vacation,' Lucy tries to get the attention of poker-playing Ricky during their stay in a Vermont cabin.

continued from page 43
an embarrassed director that the cameras hadn't been rolling. Lucy, Bill Frawley and Vivian Vance stood on the sidelines, dissolved in laughter.

In an episode entitled 'Lucy Wins a Racehorse,' guest-starring Betty Grable, Lucy wins a love-starved horse played by Tony, the best-behaved horse in Hollywood. Every time the word 'action' was said, or even whispered, Tony would immediately go through his paces—dance on his hind legs and kiss Lucy on the cheek. On one take, director Jerry Thorpe spelled out the word 'action,' jokingly testing the horse's intelligence. Thorpe gasped when the horse dutifully trotted onto the set and did his stunt. Unbeknownst to Thorpe, Bill Frawley had whispered 'Action' into Tony's ear.

In May 1958, after the fifth show, guest-starring Fernando Lamas, Desi persuaded Westinghouse—without a single test film, script or guest star, but simply on the strength of the Desilu track record—to underwrite a new concept, *The Desilu Playhouse*, for a record-breaking $12 million. The show, a one-hour special every other week, ran for two years, and featured the Ricardos and Mertzes in some episodes.

The Arnaz-Ball marriage, always troubled, was quickly deteriorating. Desi had been working constantly and putting himself under undue stress, which he then relieved by drinking to excess. Lucy became very controlled to offset Desi's lack of

At left: *Lucy consults with a production assistant as the eighth season comes to a close with the second-to-last* **I Love Lucy** *episode entitled, 'Lucy's Summer Vacation.' It is rumored that to keep the network happy, Miss Ball put her own brand of cigarettes in the sponsor's box. From the second season on, Desi took over a great deal of the directing chores in addition to his production duties. As Lucy once said when asked about the reason for the show's success, 'Desi does it all.' But the pressures of producing a half-hour of topnotch comedy became harder and harder for Desi to bear. He began to develop migraine headaches and an eye tic. William Frawley sat Desi down and said, 'Remember when you led a band? You just waved a stick and the boys took it from there. Why don't you develop a faith in others?' Once Desi began delegating a little responsibility to the people who had been hired to do these jobs, things became easier on the set.*

Below: *Desi tries to relax with a game of tennis. 'I quit the business in 1961 because it got to be a monster. At the beginning it was fun, but when you're in charge of three studios, with three thousand people and 35 soundstages working all the time, the fun is long gone.'*

Opposite page: *Desi, Jr and Lucie Arnaz meet up with a couple of Santas.*

At left: *Ricky's vacation is wearing him out.*

Below, left: *Halfway through the sixth season, Lucy and Ricky decided to leave their Manhattan brownstone for the 'country' of Westport, Connecticut. The dog, named after Fred Mertz, was given to Little Ricky in the previous episode.*

Opposite page: *Lucy rehearses her lines with Ethel Mertz for the annual Yankee Doodle Day Celebration.*

The real Arnaz children made their one and only **I Love Lucy** *appearance on the last half-hour episode ever filmed (aired 6 May 1957), 'The Ricardos Dedicate a Statue.' However, Desi, Jr, aged four, and Lucie, aged five and a half, were seen only in the crowd scene.*

control. She was tired of his philandering. Their legendary fighting was upsetting Lucie and Desi, Jr, who were now old enough to show the deleterious effects of dueling parents. Desi and Lucy, one of Hollywood's favorite and most famous couples, separated.

Lucy filed for the divorce, citing Desi's drinking, tantrums and infidelities. She referred to him as a 'Jekyll and Hyde'. As previously agreed by the couple, Desi did not contest her testimony. He did, however, make a statement in which he said that he didn't deny the charges only because he wanted the divorce to happen more quickly.

One month before the divorce, CBS cancelled *The Desilu*

Playhouse, the last vestige of their collaboration. The couple concluded their 19-year career as co-producers and co-stars with the 193d Lucy and Ricky episode, entitled 'Lucy Meets the Moustache,' co-starring Ernie Kovacs.

On 4 May 1960, a judge awarded Lucy an uncontested divorce, and then split Desilu Studios—then worth $20 million—evenly between them. Lucy kept their Beverly Hills mansion, the two cars and their cemetery plot at Forest Lawn. Desi retained the membership in the Thunderbird Country Club in Palm Springs, a truck, a golf cart, 11 racehorses, and their ranch at Riverside. The two children received $450 monthly support apiece from Desi.

The town of Westport is celebrating Yankee Doodle Day, commemorating their Revolutionary War ancestors with a monument for which Ricky is responsible. When Lucy showed Ethel the stone sculpture of a patriot kneeling with a musket, Little Ricky announced that Fred, his dog, had run away again.

Lucy jumped in the station wagon and zoomed off, forgetting about the trailer bearing the statue in the back, and destroying the one-of-a-kind sculpture.

Opposite page and below: As a stand-in for the broken statue, Lucy impersonates a Minuteman at the unveiling of the statue—until Fred the dog licks her face.

At right: Lucy is prepared by a makeup man for her impersonation of a statue.

Keep Your Eye On The Ball

In an effort to keep busy, Lucy immediately made a movie called *The Facts of Life* with Bob Hope, and then went to New York to be in a Broadway play. The project with her old friend was supposed to be therapeutic after her traumatic divorce, but Desi visited often to see the children, not allowing Lucy's old wounds to heal.

After *I Love Lucy* ended its original airing schedule on 24 September 1961, Vivian Vance moved to Connecticut and remarried. She was ready to retire, until Lucy flew out for a visit with a script in hand. Lucy, too, had recently remarried, to a comedian named Gary Morton.

When rehearsals commenced for the new show, Desi was on hand with a good luck jade clover and a kiss on the cheek for Lucy. He even produced *The Lucy Show* for Desilu until his retirement. The show lasted six years on CBS, in the old *I Love Lucy* Monday night time slot. Lucy Carmichael and her two children clowned — with Vivian next door — for three seasons. *The Danny Thomas Show*, *The Untouchables*, *Ben Casey*, *Lassie*, *The Andy Griffith Show*, *The Dick Van Dyke Show*, *My Three Sons* and *My Favorite Martian* were just some of the successful productions from the Desilu stable.

Shortly after the premiere of *The Lucy Show* in 1962, Desi told Lucy that he wanted to retire, so Lucy bought out his share of Desilu Productions for over $2.5 million. Desi retreated to his horse ranch in Corona, California, and married redheaded Edith Mack Hirsch, who bore great

resemblance to Lucy. Several years later, he came out of retirement to found Desi Arnaz Productions, which produced *The Mothers-in-Law*, starring Eve Arden and Kaye Ballard. The show was created by none other than Madelyn Pugh and Bob Carroll, Jr, creators and writers for the original *I Love Lucy*.

William Frawley immediately accepted an offer to play Bub on *My Three Sons*. Five years into the series, Frawley's health began to fail, and he retired. On 3 March 1966, he died of a heart attack while strolling on Hollywood Boulevard. His last television appearance was a guest shot on *The Lucy Show*. He had remarked to a reporter just before his death, 'I love that girl. I've loved her since she was a star-struck kid at RKO.'

In 1967, Lucy began to consider bids on the production company, but her reluctance to yield her company to someone else made her impossibly particular about choosing the buyer. When at last she sold the company to Gulf + Western, she was at once horrified, depressed and relieved. She made millions of dollars and was suddenly released from great responsibility and pressure, but she had also lost the institution that she and Desi had built together during the previous 16 years. She plunged herself back into her work, making the film *Yours, Mine and Ours* with Henry Fonda.

In 1974, she began to consider ending *Here's Lucy*. Her health was poor, and although the show was still popular, the CBS

officials concurred that it was time to discontinue the show — perhaps because of Lucy's increasing ill-tempered treatment of her stagehands, staff and network executives. Always demanding the most from herself and everyone around her, she was exhausted. Still, she refused to officially 'retire' — she referred to her professional status as 'tapered off.'

Her semi-retirement in 1976 called for two CBS specials a year. In 1976, there was a two-hour 25th Anniversary show in her honor, featuring clips and interviews with Lucy and with superstars with whom Lucy worked during the years. In 1979, Lucy moved to NBC, breaking her 28-year association with CBS because, she said, she was 'tired of doing nothing.' She mounted a special in January 1980 called 'Lucy Moves to NBC.'

Above: As a businesswoman, Lucy was a formidable power, but socially, Lucy was always a gracious hostess.

Opposite page: In 1961, Lucy returned to television with **The Lucy Show**. The show lasted until 1968, when Lucy came out with **Here's Lucy**, starring her own two children.

These pages: *Lucy co-starred with her old friend Bob Hope in the 1960 movie* **The Facts of Life**. *They had co-starred in two other films,* **Sorrowful Jones** *and* **Fancy Pants**.

In September 1981, Lucy's net worth was listed by *Los Angeles* magazine as between $50 million and $100 million. She spent a great deal of time with her daughter Lucie Arnaz's family—her husband, actor Laurence Luckinbill, and two sons, Simon and Joseph—even renting an apartment in the East Sixties of Manhattan to be near them.

She received many honors in her final years. On 26 February 1984, Lucy was among the first to be inducted into the Television Hall of Fame. The others included Milton Berle, Paddy Chayefsky, Edward R Murrow, David Sarnoff, Norman Lear and William S Paley. In April of that same year, she was honored by the Museum of Broadcasting in Manhattan.

She and Gary Morton became involved in the running of Lucille Ball Productions, which presented the movie *All the Right*
continued on page 63

59

Opposite page: In her long career, Lucy worked with lions, tigers, goats, penguins, a bull, chimpanzees, porpoises, horses, bears, cats, birds, pigs, dogs and children. Fortunately for Lucy, this gorilla is just a man in a suit.

At right: John Wayne appeared on **I Love Lucy** in a two-part show entitled 'Lucy and John Wayne' in 1955. Wayne's movie, **Blood Alley**, was plugged incessantly throughout the two shows, though Wayne appeared only in the second part. Wayne returned to appear on **Here's Lucy**.

Below, left: In **Here's Lucy**, Lucy played a widow in search of gainful employment. A stint as a waitress in a drive-in restaurant sends her scurrying to an employment agency owned by Sammy Davis, Jr **(below, right)**, who was another real life friend of Lucille Ball.

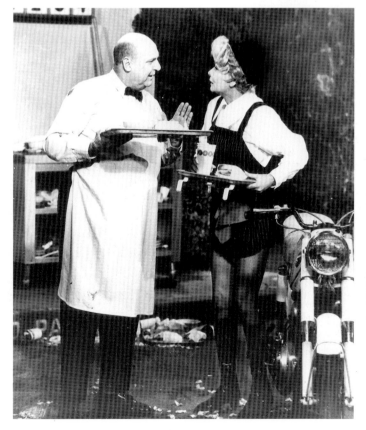

At left: Lucy joins her friend Carol Burnett in the role of the cleaning lady on **The Carol Burnett Show**.

Below: Gale Gordon has Ball in 'chains.'

Opposite page: Lucy, approaching 60 years old and perennially hip, does the frug.

Opposite page: *Lucy and Vivian disguised as geisha girls. In her career, Lucy 'disguised' herself as an Indian, a bricklayer, a grape stomper, a fight manager, a sax player in a band of nuns, a Martian, an astronaut, a pool hustler, a kangaroo, the front end of a horse, a pickle, and a meter maid (**right**).*

Below, right: *Vivian Vance still lived next door, and Lucy's co-star of the 1940s, Gale Gordon (**far right**), also became a regular on **The Lucy Show**.*

continued from page 57
Moves, starring Tom Cruise. Lucy had protested against the sex and violence in movies and television since the early 1960s, and she did something about it, by making family entertainment such as *Mame, Yours, Mine and Ours* and *All the Right Moves*.

In 1984, despite having said that she was never going to work in television again, Lucy went to work starring in a teleplay entitled *Stone Pillow*, in which she played a bag lady, and in the fall of 1986 began a show for ABC called *Life With Lucy*. She was saddened when the show was cancelled due to bad ratings, but just a month later, on 17 December, she was honored by President Ronald Reagan at the Kennedy Center in Washington, DC with an award for life-long achievement.

Less than a year later, Lucy was dead at the age of 77. The people to whom she had brought so much laughter were now brought to tears. The world's greatest comedienne, her grandpa's Lucyball, who had started in vaudeville, been a model, a Ziegfeld girl, a star of radio, movies, stage and television, left behind a legion of fans and an enormous body of work for them to cherish. Generations of children not yet born when any of the Lucy shows were originally aired are now discovering in syndication the wacky housewife. She will forever remain the Lucy that everyone loves.

64

At left: Lucy with Gale Gordon. Gale had been an integral part of Lucy's career since they appeared in a series of movies together in the early 1940s. A part of Lucy's radio show **My Favorite Husband** from 1948 until 1951, Gale was badly wanted for the part of Fred Mertz, but instead he appeared in **I Love Lucy** as Ricky's boss at the Tropicana. Here he is shown during his eleven-year stint as Lucy's boss, Mr Mooney, on **The Lucy Show** (1963-1968) and **Here's Lucy** (1968-1974.)

Below, left: Lucy starred with her own two children, Desi, Jr and Lucie Arnaz, in the 1968 show, **Here's Lucy**.

Opposite page: After **I Love Lucy**, Lucy was busy with her charities, her television show, her movies, and the running of Desilu Productions.

HHT-16

In **Yours, Mine and Ours** (1968), Lucy played a widow with eight children (**below**), who marries a widower (Henry Fonda, **at left**) with 10 children. Based on the true story of Frank and Helen Beardsley, a Northern California couple, the story follows their marriage, their attempts to peacefully combine their families, and their decision to have more children together (**at right, center**).

The film was a success, grossing over $17 million, and Lucy greatly enjoyed working with Fonda on an equal footing (**at right, top**); she had been a bit player in his 1942 film, **The Big Street**. The scene in which the children feed Lucy liquor until she's drunk, or in which her false eyelashes climb up onto her forehead, are priceless.

A young Tim Matheson played the eldest boy; he can be seen peering over Henry Fonda's shoulder at the wedding and in uniform greeting the first 'ours'. Suzanne Cupito (who grew up to be television actress Morgan Brittany) and a very young Tracy Nelson are also in the cast.

Opposite page: *Lucy, ever lovely, appeared on 33 television specials, including those of friends Gene Kelly, Jackie Gleason, Danny Kaye, Ed Sullivan, Henry Fonda, Jimmy Stewart, Bob Hope and Milton Berle. Lucy was interviewed on Barbara Walters, roasted by Dean Martin, and even appeared on* **The Second Annual Circus of the Stars** *(1977).*

At right: *Lucy has adventures in* **Lucille Ball in London** *(aired 24 October 1966 on CBS).*

Below: *Richard Burton and Elizabeth Taylor were among the many famous people who appeared on* **Here's Lucy**.

At left: Lucy often appeared on **The Carol Burnett Show**, which ran from 1966 to 1978. Here, Carol and Lucy are 1920s-style flappers.

Below: Lucy was in demand on the talk show circuit. She made occassional appearances on Dinah Shore's program.

Opposite page: Lucy worked with many different charities, including the Lung Association.

Opposite page: *Lucy as Mame. In 1973, Lucy plunged into the making of* **Mame**, *based on Patrick Dennis' book,* **Auntie Mame**, *and on the Broadway play. With the exception of* **Wildcat!** *in 1960, Lucy hadn't danced in a movie for 30 years. She went into intensive training with Onna White, who had choreographed* **Oliver!**, *getting up at five in the morning for months to begin her workout. Lucy said of the experience, 'It was hell! I thought I'd die. It's a miracle what Onna White did with me.'*

At right, above: *Lucy with second husband, Gary Morton. After their marriage on 19 November 1961, she said, 'I didn't want to get married again [before meeting Gary]. I didn't think I would find a mature, adult person like Gary, a really understanding guy who is wonderful to be around and uncomplicated.' His devotion to her was obvious to everyone.*

At right, below: *Lucy and friend at a March of Dimes fundraiser.*

74

At left: Lucy waves to fans outside the soundstage where **Mame** was filmed.

Below: Lucy with **Mame** co-star Kirby Furlong.

Opposite page: Lucy's role in **Mame** was far more glamorous than her previous musical role in **Wildcat!**. When Lucy was nearing 50 years old, she had decided to finance and star in a musical about a female wildcatter in the southeastern United States oil fields at the turn of the century. The show opened in Philadelphia and moved to New York's Alvin Theatre, drawing huge crowds of Lucy's fans.

The highlight of **Wildcat!** for Lucy was when Mousy, the Yorkshire terrier in the show, relieved himself right on stage in the middle of a scene. Lucy grabbed a mop and pail from supporting cast members and cleaned up the mess, explaining to the audience in a mock apology for the interruption, 'It's in the small print of my contract.'

Opposite page: Lucy's second husband, comedian Gary Morton, was an inveterate golfer, so Lucy spent a lot time in golf carts.

At right: On 17 December 1984, she was honored by President Reagan at the Kennedy Center in Washington, DC with an award for life-long achievement.

Below: Lucy with her pals (**from left**) Bob Hope, Lucy, Milton Berle, Angie Dickinson and Lee Marvin.

Filmography
Movies

Broadway Thru a Keyhole (1933)
Blood Money (1933)
Roman Scandals (1933)
Moulin Rouge (1933)
Nana (1934)
Bottoms Up (1934)
Hold That Girl (1934)
Bulldog Drummond Strikes Back (1934)
The Affairs of Cellini (1934)
Kid Millions (1934)
Broadway Bill (1934)
Jealousy (1934)
Men of the Night (1934)
Fugitive Lady (1934)
Carnival (1935)*
Roberta (1935)
Old Man Rhythm (1935)
Top Hat (1935)
The Three Musketeers (1935)
I Dream Too Much (1935)
Chatterbox (1936)
Follow the Fleet (1936)
The Farmer in the Dell (1936)
Bunker Bean (1936)
That Girl From Paris (1936)
Don't Tell the Wife (1937)
Stage Door (1937)
Joy of Living (1938)
Go Chase Yourself (1938)
Having a Wonderful Time (1938)
The Affairs of Annabel (1938)
Room Service (1938)
The Next Time I Marry (1938)
Annabel Takes a Tour (1938)
Beauty For the Asking (1939)
Twelve Crowded Hours (1939)
Panama Lady (1939)
Five Came Back (1939)

That's Right You're Wrong (1939)
The Marines Fly High (1940)
You Can't Fool Your Wife (1940)
Dance Girl Dance (1940)
Too Many Girls (1940)
A Guy, a Girl and a Gob (1940)
Look Who's Laughing (1941)
Valley of the Sun (1942)
The Big Street (1942)
Seven Days Leave (1942)
DuBarry Was a Lady (1943)
Best Foot Forward (1943)
Thousands Cheer (1943)
Meet the People (1944)
Without Love (1945)
Abbott and Costello in Hollywood (1945)
Ziegfeld Follies (1946)
The Dark Corner (1946)
Easy to Wed (1946)
Two Smart People (1946)
Lover Come Back (1946)
Lured (1947)
Her Husband's Affairs (1947)
Sorrowful Jones (1949)
Easy Living (1949)
Miss Grant Takes Richmond (1949)
Fancy Pants (1950)
The Fuller Brush Girl (1950)
The Magic Carpet (1950)
The Long, Long Trailer (1954)
Forever Darling (1956)
The Facts of Life (1960)
Critic's Choice (1963)
A Guide For the Married Man (1967)
Yours, Mine and Ours (1968)
Mame (1973)
Stone Pillow (television) (1985)

* first billed role

Television

I Love Lucy (1951-55)
The Lucy Show (1962-68)
Here's Lucy (1968-73)
Life With Lucy (1986)

Above: In the 1985 teleplay **Stone Pillow**, Lucy played a feisty bag lady in New York City. Lucy lost 23 pounds she could ill afford to lose and collapsed from dehydration as a result of wearing heavy winter costumes in the heat.

Lucy said of her dramatic performance, 'Because of [**Stone Pillow**] I have learned to have compassion for the homeless. And I hope you will buy it. I hope you people will let me do something besides **Lucy**. If you think, "I don't want to see her do that; I want to see her be funny," I can buy that. But I hope you'll think [**Stone Pillow**] has some merit.'

Index